Can You See What I Said?

T. H. Speaks

BookLeaf
Publishing

India | USA | UK

Can You See What I Said?

© 2024 T.H. Speaks

Presentation by *BookLeaf Publishing*

Web: www.bookleafpub.com

E-mail: info@bookleafpub.com

ISBN: 9789358315486

First edition 2024

DEDICATION

This book is dedicated to my Circle who always has a way of ensuring I know they are always with me.

It is also dedicated to all of the people constantly trying to make the world a better place.

ACKNOWLEDGEMENT

I want to acknowledge the people and/or events that caused me to write this book.

It took your hate and ignorance for my voice to be heard.

PREFACE

Dear Readers,

I wrote this book for each of you. I am putting words to the tragedy's occurring around us.

I hope you can see what I said as you read this book and then I hope you find ways to be the change this world needs.

T.H.

I Want to Scream

I can discuss the Dove commercial and how it's so blatantly racist. I can discuss how Dove managed to convey in its commercial that being African American is dirty but they can cleanse you of the filth.

I can discuss how this commercial forces me to explain to my daughters and sons how they are not dirty. I have to explain to them that they are wonderfully made. I have to come up with some explanation that explains the ignorance of the commercial while not hardening their hearts to the people on this earth. I have to try to help them to continue to see good. I am forced to explain all of this when I truly just want to scream.

I'm so tired of the closet racists coming out of their closets and creating messes for us to clean up. I want to scream because I'm tired of people pretending that their isn't a very serious racial problem in America. I want to scream because people continue to tell me that we are just overly sensitive.

I want to scream because it's my children, your children, their children, our children that continue to be hurt by the racism.

I want to scream because people want to pretend that they are outraged at Colin Kaepernick because he's disrespecting the men and women of the military and yet they still refuse to address the reasons he says that he's kneeling.

I want to scream because people continue to say how far we've come and that we, as in African Americans, should just be happy and stop complaining but when I look around I wonder what are they seeing.

You see when I look around I see minorities still being treated differently than others. I get it. It's not the 1600s, 1700s, 1800s, 1950s, 1960s, etc. It's 2017 and we should be far beyond Martin's dream. But we aren't. In ways we are living Martin's, Malcolm's, Medgar's, Rosa's and every of other person who protested, marched, sat, kneeled, stood, died, went to jail, etc worst nightmare.

We are free but yet we aren't. We have voting rights but we have to go back and get permission to use them every 50 years. We aren't lynched

from trees or made to pick cotton. No there's a
new name for it. They are called prisons.

Slave labor! Free labor! Now it's justified by
these things called laws created by people whose
hearts are questionable and are driven by greed.
Laws in a justice system that is supposed to be
blind and equal; however, the statistics make
you realize that it can't be true. How can it be
when African Americans make up the majority
of the prison population yet we are the minority
of the country's population?

Treat them like a game of baseball. Three strikes
and you are out except the only people that get
walks, fouls, home runs, on base hits, or grand
slams don't look like us.

Every time one of us are up to bat, there's no
doubt that it's a strike about to be had. It has us
so messed up that we find ourselves celebrating
what we call victories. You know these victories.
We have to celebrate acquittals that shouldn't
have been and they too are based off the color of
the skin.

If we say our lives matter, someone interjects
that all lives matter but know one wants to
acknowledge that all lives don't matter because

if they did there would be no need to explain the meaning behind our statement.

We have to apologize for being African American. We have to apologize for being tired. We have to apologize for wanting equal rights. We have to apologize for wanting a seat at the table instead of just accepting the crumbs. We have to apologize when you realize we aren't dumb. We have to apologize for loving our skin and heritage. We have to apologize for daring to want every day to be just as black as it is white. I mean after all, you did give us February without a fight.

Go ahead and pretend that everything is okay. Tonight when you put your child to bed what will you speak? You know what I'll do before I go in my prayer closet and weep? I'll hug and kiss each of my children just like you. Then I'll have to look my children in the eyes and lie. I'll lie because the truth will break their spirits or strip their innocence away in ways that I don't want to think about. I'll lie because the truth will make them question everything we ever taught them. I'll lie because the truth is a burden I don't want them to bear. I'll lie because the truth may change them from being the good people they are to being looked upon as statistics.

You know the statistics that are used to determine what their future should be. You know the statistics that are used to justify the racists beliefs. The ones that don't include my children being better than you and me.

So yes, I'll lie because I refuse to give you the opportunity to write my children off. They will defy your odds and your expectations. They will. Even if it takes my last breath to make it happen. They will make Dove rethink their commercials. They'll make the statisticians wonder, "How in the hell did we make this blunder?"

But please know this.... I lie to my children to protect my children but don't come for my children because I'm not my children.

Peaks and Summits

I am laying here on the floor with this ball in my hand reminiscing on how that young boy became THIS MAN!!!

I remember how many times I hurt and cried. I wondered if there was truth in the lies but then I would look into my mother's eyes as she said over and over again "Keep going, TreVon. You are destined to fly."

The boy who loved math and was always business minded.

I want to thank my teacher Ms. Bean for seeing the greatness in me even when my third grade classmate could not appreciate I was already starting on my journey towards my destiny.

Lived in the Hills not because of black flight but because there was more I needed to mold me into the person I would become and expose those who I now understand feared the young black boy who would one day become A Life Changing Young Black Man.

They saw the light that was already to bright to be denied so they did and said everything they could in hopes of it being destroyed.

Thanks to the math teacher, who is not worthy of being named, who called my mother to say "But but but blacks are not on the math team."

I do not think she understood that she called my mother, my supporter, my encourager, my cheerleader, my defender, my ride or die and my biggest fan.

She made her first mistake, in regards to me, with that call because as far as my mother was concerned she had lost her mind.

You see this teacher chose the wrong child with the right parent who was unafraid of racists white folks and when it came to her child it was not about if she had time because she was going to handle it.

She laughed at her on the phone, as if the teacher told a joke, and told her "I will see you and your principal tomorrow and by the time I am finished you will call me '74 Ali using the Rope A Dope.

This was not the art of war. Oh no it was even worse because she had just hurt my mother's child and everyone knew there would be no mercy.

Those two teachers who said I was not in line when GOD gave out brains.

My name was further up the list than either of yours so you probably could not see from the nosebleed section all HE gave me.

HE gave me: A level of intelligence that is indescribable. The talents and gifts are astonishing. The heart full of love is a level of peace you will never understand. I could keep going but I will leave it at the heart because I understand you never received anything else. HE is still trying to work on those for you.

Remember how the two of you went out of your way to make every day painful for me?

You bullied a middle school child and believed it was an okay way to be…

I remember the days of sitting silent while you talked about me to the entire class.

Today, I really want to simply say "Kiss my ass." but I need all the other little black boys and little black girls to understand you did not win.

My mother was in tune with me so she knew there was a problem but I would not tell her so she could solve it.

She was fighting this school system on all levels.

Systemic oppression was just the beginning. They did anything to make people think they were winning when they were just a bunch of old white folks with shriveled up hearts who was trying to hang on to those distant relations with their great great grandparents who owned slave plantations.

They could not understand these new generations that was okay with everyone winning and did not hide their sexual orientation.

This generation did not believe in hiding skeletons in the closets and under the bed so when they found out Uncle John was a pedophile it was not going to be a family secret so they went out and told instead.

This generation messed them up because they wanted us to look down when speaking to them but we looked them square in the eyes because the only thing that separated us was the hate they carried around for all of us.

I remember the morning as if it is happening now.

My mother is following the carpool line to drop me off. I look over and see one of you as you walk with your daughter up the hill to the school where lots racists people are getting paid.

I start trembling and crying not realizing my mother sensed the change in me.

She stopped the vehicle and made me tell it all.

I told her real fast hoping she would just let it pass but it was not to be.

Even I understood how much my mother loved me.

What happened next taught me many things…

My mother drove on up the hill to where you were in your perfect little world.

She put the car in park, let down the window and opened the door never caring that all of the Hills was about to understand that she truly was unmoved by them.

Do you remember that morning?

She called your name loudly twice and had the carpool lanes blocked while trying to contain her rage.

You looked over at her and smiled as she told you the conversation was about her child.

It was not until she gave you my name that you understood it was hitting the fan and this woman was taking no pity on the person who called himself a man.

She started her conversation with you right there in front of your daughter.

Do you remember what you did?

You sputtered "If if if if you want to set up a conference, you can call the office."

She came right back and said "Yes, I can but I am not. There is no time like the present to sort this out."

You looked around hoping someone would come to your rescue and she looked around wishing someone would try.

Do you remember what happened next?

I do…

I thought you could fly.

You sprinted, I thought you were going to leave your daughter behind you were moving so fast, and said "ma'am, please call the office for a conference."

Off you flew and ran straight into the building.

This little woman I loved became a giant in so many ways but I also was worried it was about to be a long day.

I was angry at her too because what she did was sure to make them mad and all that meant was they were about to find new ways to hurt me in and out of class.

They were already stealing all my dreams.

This ball that I am holding now was not even allowed by me on the school team.

These were my dreams did she not understand. I was at the point of just trying to survive it.

What did she mean I am destined to be THAT MAN?

It was as if she could feel my fear, anger, frustrations and my willingness to just let them win.

She turned around, looked at me and said "You do not hide anything from me. I do not care what it is about or even if you think I will not agree with you. I am your protector. Now understand this will be handled. If they say anything, call or text me immediately. I will be here in three minutes."

She put the car in drive and pulled up to the drop off area as if she was not preparing to deal with more systemic issues that this school was definitely founded on.

Her phone started ringing as I was about to get out the vehicle. I watched her decline it twice without even looking at who was calling because her concern was me.

The third time she accepted the call and it played through the Bluetooth. I was shocked to hear who was on the phone. Someone was calling to set up a conference. The teacher ran in the school and said "My mother confronted him in carpool about something regarding her son."

My mother leaned over, gave me a hug and kiss, told me to have a great day because she has this…

I heard her say "Set the meeting for today in one hour."

Every time I hear someone say "What's a goon to a goblin?"

I laugh because my mother showed me those goons were nothing to her and she has a zero tolerance policy when it comes to her children.

Now, I was not in either meeting with either teacher (yes, she met with them both) but my

mother has one rule when dealing with people
she believes she is unable to trust…

KEEP RECEIPTS!!!

It is a must.

I really do pity anyone who ever forces the most
loyal person I know to cut him or her off
because you tried her or even worse, someone
she loves or someone who is defenseless.

Between the receipts and patience she possesses,
it is guaranteed there is going to be a reckoning
when she is ready for it.

Back to those meetings…

I have listened to them numerous times over the
years because they remind me of how cowards
operate.

The teacher from carpool apologized, cried, tried
to justify and threw anything else at the wall he
thought would stick (it was jokes, all in fun and
he tried to stop the other teacher several times
when he thought he went overboard including
when he said I was a waste of space).

My mother showed him no mercy and he understood, by the end of the meeting, it was not finished.

He did come up to me that morning, with tears in his eyes, as he apologized. He said he did not know he was hurting me.

I heard him out. I explained if he was the adult and did not know then he may need more education.

The second teacher initially tried to be a jerk. Maybe he saw the first one leave in tears.

Honestly, I believe the first teacher received the lighter side of my mother (if that was possible).

The second teacher was definitely reduced to nothing by the time the conference was over. It was as if he walked into the room but there was nobody left when she was finished with him to leave it.

My mother met with the assistant principal who is still a part of our village today.

An advocate who still refuses to do it any way but the right way.

I am proud of you because you finally received
the recognition you deserved long before you
actually were awarded it.

You stood for the right things and they could not
accept it.

I want to name you but I am respecting your
position.

My mother met with the principal and then she
went right to the superintendent.

She kept going.

The Hills will continue decline until they change
their hearts. Nothing will ever last there as long
as you refuse to change.

FYI: Trump election signs hanging on the walls
of your rooms in a public school, allowing
children to be told they are going to be slaves
again and deported is a problem.

They thought they would tire my mother. She
did not bend or break.

She truly became '74 Ali with the Rope A Dope.

Years of battling.

The one thing my mother wanted to make sure I understood as I listened to every recording was they never challenged my intelligence, talents, gifts or the fact they knew I was going to soar high in life.

She made sure I heard the ignorant justifications, the fear of my success especially when their own children did not possess my abilities and the love I had surrounding me by some.

She made sure I understood their system was structured to only use other people's talents to make their own shine.

If you refuse to comply, they will attempt to convince you that you lack in areas when truthfully you are more than enough.

Then she looked me in the eyes and said "TreVon, you are an Eagle. You are destined to soar majestically above them. They are buzzards. They feed off of dead things. Eagles and buzzards do not fly together. Now refuse to let these buzzards get in your head. I will handle the buzzards. Go soar, Son. Go soar."

As I lay here with this ball in my hand, I am reflecting on what she just said to me. "TreVon, you are an Eagle. You are destined to soar majestically above them. They are buzzards. They feed off of dead things. Eagles and buzzards do not fly together. Now refuse to let these buzzards get in your head. I will handle the buzzards. Go soar, Son. Go soar. Remember, if the world gets cold and you ever feel the desire to come home to me, always know my arms are wide open. You have a key. The lights will be on and your room will be waiting. I will cook your favorite foods. We can talk about it or just watch Red. Stay as long as you want to stay and when you feel it is time, I will understand you must be on your way. I will hug you tight, kiss your cheek and tears will flow down my face as I watch as you walk back into your destiny. Son, I am opening up my hands and releasing yours because Son, you have become That Man and even more."

To all of the black children let this be a lesson. There will always be storms but the beautiful weather afterwards is for you!!!

Believe in yourself even if others doubt you.

Go to the ones you can trust and tell them if
something is wrong.

They will fight for you because they will refuse
to let you give up.

If you do not know anyone else, drop me your
name.

I will send it to my mother and I promise your
life will change.

She has some real friends who are family too
and they will go to battle for each and every one
of you.

Here is the thing, I will be there to fight for
you!!!

The peaks and summits I am reaching are great
but it is the valleys I will not forget.

Look up, Little One. Do not be scared.

That is just me reaching out my hand.

Grab it and I will pull you up until you no longer
need my strength.

But please do not doubt me, I got your back
100%!!!

I will give you the gift that has been given to
me.

People who are there for me even when I am
unable to see them.

They hit the heart button on social media, they
send a text, put up a post, inbox me, comment on
my posts, call me, send unexpected CashApps or
do nothing that I am able to visibly see.

I just know they are always there watching over
me.

-T.H.-

A Note from the Author and His Mother

I wrote several short stories based on a picture of
my son.

I saw the picture and it spoke to me in so many
ways.

They would not stop coming.

Each and every short story is based on my interpretation of what my son is thinking as he lays there or is about to dunk the ball after taking it through his legs.

Visually I see my son. I see a mountain with valleys, peaks, summits, storms and sunshine.

Some are serious and others are lighthearted. If you know my son then you will also recognize some are definitely TNasty too.

This one holds me in a different space. I understand why which is the reason for the tears streaming down my face.

The short stories will not be released nor am I certain you will ever see the picture that gave me the desire to write them.

If you are reading this story, it is because my son has chosen to share it.

So many people believe he is just a silly kid who is always smiling.

Please do not misunderstand his classic response "Life is good." to your inquiry of how is he doing.

It has always been bigger than basketball.

He has worked for everything he has in life and
to become THAT MAN!!!

If he is smiling, it is not because he does not
have things going on. It is because he chooses to
brighten up the days for others and deal with his
own things internally.

He is deeper than the ocean and if you do not
know it, you are not a part of the people who
matter.

As his mother, I always know.

This Isn't The Dream

He had a dream but this isn't the dream.

This is a nightmare!!!

It's impossible to explain to anyone who isn't living this nightmare how anxious, hopeful but prepared we are for whatever happens in Kenosha today.

Say this name for me… Jacob Blake

His name brings so many emotions up for POC. His name brings so many words to mind but JUSTICE isn't one of them.

Say this name for me… Kyle Rittenhouse and follow it up with murderer, criminal and evader of the true justice he deserves.

POC are already braced for what will happen.

We recognize that those fake white tears he shed is a part of the show put on to turn this real crime into a story of "a great kid who was forced to…"

It doesn't even matter that he chose to go there with weapons because in America only POC are truly guilty even before they are found guilty.

POC will receive harsh sentences without a doubt but the system will find ways to create lesser charges for those who are guilty of heinous crimes only because the people who committed the crimes look just like the people who designed this flawed system.

Please don't point to this as just a political issue.

Did you all miss the statement where Biden said "It's hard to be a policeman today."

Damn Joe, IT HAS BEEN HARD TO BE A PERSON OF COLOR FOREVER!!!

Never mind, he also thought Derek Chauvin's sentence was "fair".

I won't go further down the road by expounding on the bills he's helped to pass that harmed our communities specifically.

It's not all political. It's a heart issue. It's a racism issue. It's a realization that if all things are equitable POC will soar.

No matter what happens when this verdict is delivered, POC already understand what we must do after hearing it.

We will feel all of the emotions which the verdict will provoke and afterwards, we must still keep going as if we are blind to the injustices because the next one is not too far behind it.

Please pay attention to the Ahmaud Arbery trial.

I'm going to silence this blue app until after the verdict because I understand someone is going to mess up and say the wrong thing.

I realize when you do if I see it I'm not going to hold my tongue and I promise you I'm going to stand on what I said while more than likely telling you what you can do with your feelings.

The reality is you get the luxury of feeling while POC live it!!!

Living

The days are full

The nights are short

Questioning myself over life choices.

Standing still

Recalling options

The work of two

Condensed into one

Ensuring it is never felt

By the little ones.

Feeling tired

Meeting complete

Need to sleep

At times feeling weak

Recalling the nights of crying myself to sleep

Time to refocus

Take a deep breath

Looking at the trail from my office to the spot I am currently standing.

The shoes remind me of the path I chose in life.

The jacket represents the protection in place for them.

The hair pins now laying on the top shelf tell me I made it to the time when I can finally let my hair down and just be…

Then I hear the most beautiful voice and it says "Mommy, your bed please."

The doubts fade

Everything falls into place.

I snuggle him extra tight

Walk into the next room for more snuggles with her.

Lots of giggles

Pretending I am not going to give in

Before telling them to get one book each

Watching as they each carefully select their choice

Smiling because they understand one of their choices they will read to me

Studying them as they study their books

I see their amazingness

I see them without thinking about others

I want to hug them a little tighter

Books found and pajama night declared

We head to my room

Put them in and discuss the rules

I grab my things so I can shower

Right now I do not get a few hours

By the time I finish

I hear them reading together

These beautiful Lights shining brightly in my
life forever

My heart is free

Love is fierce

Smiling because some things truly are priceless

Put on my pajamas and join my crew

Halfway through the first book sleep has
claimed them

I slip in some kisses and grab the books

Go pick up my trail and put everything away.

Standing there drinking some water and looking
at a screen

I see my blessings

Life has delivered some heartache but this is not
it

This…

This…

This…

IS LIVING and I am doing it!!!

#MommyMemories
#Joy
#Blessings
#Love
#Peace

Where Do We Really Go From Here?

I would like to say I was traumatized the day *45 encouraged domestic terrorists to attack the Capitol Building.

I want to say I was shocked and I lost my hope in America that day.

I'm unable to say these things because it's not true.

I watched them play the video at the opening of *45's impeachment trial and I still didn't feel the emotions I wanted to feel.

I'm angry that I'm unable to have those feelings!!!

I'm angry that the injustices committed against black people in this country have been so atrocious that I'm unable to feel what all of us should feel over these crimes against Americans.

Yet when I think about it, I'm reminded that
America doesn't consider me an equal nor does
it care about me.

I'm reminded that politicians use us for our
votes and their needs. They leave us with
promises that are never fulfilled.

They murder us for crimes that they created and
not ones we committed.

They imprison us to continue slavery under the
disguise of incarceration which is somehow
supposed to lead to rehabilitation.

They refuse to bring in the social workers,
educators, mental health workers, livable wages,
excellent schools, all encompassing health care
and other necessary tools to deter poverty which
would cause poor communities to thrive instead
of die.

Crime would decrease but that would affect their
investment in the private prison systems they
continue to build to pile more black people
inside them.

America was built on the backs and with the hands of black people who didn't have any choices.

Now, here we are hundreds of years later, still without a choice.

Why am I unable to feel the level of dismay that others feel over the actions of Americans?

Why am I unable to feel anything until I see the black police officer put his life on the line for people who won't ever put their political careers nor their lives on the line for him?

Why am I crying as I watch him risk his life but I'm unable to form the words to tell him not to do it?

Why am I angry that he loves America in ways that America does not love him?

Why do I see the faces of not just my ancestors, Martin, Malcolm, Megar, Rosa, Coretta and those who came before me but the faces of Sandra, Trayvon, Ahmaud, George, Philando, instead of the faces of the terrorists who are actually violating this country?

Why do I feel as if America stole something from me before I ever truly possessed it?

Why am I not weeping for America but I am instead weeping for black people?

Why am I screaming Breonna and gasping for breath because I hear George saying "I can't breathe."?

Why am I not feeling?

Cowards

Cowards operate from their positions in life which include manipulation and fear.

They manipulate people and situations in an attempt to make themselves look better.

They operate exactly as they are in their real lives… COWARDS

They create dissension, destroy relationships, cause anger, enjoy watching hurt all around them and act as if they are not doing it.

They will gaslight you into believing it is not them.

When it all hits the fan, watch them go quiet or make carefully crafted statements.

They are afraid of missing out on their end goal so they just remain cowards.

They allow others to take the blame and be the bad person.

When you see them, recognize them and expose them.

Save yourself the time and energy it takes to try to help or heal them.

They will destroy you too!!!

Deliberately…

People think if you stay humble and move silently they may treat you any way they desire.

Someone may want to explain my humbleness is because the work and people are all that matter to me. I am humble because I am able to use my talents and gifts towards a greater purpose.

I move in silence because I accomplish more which means the people benefit.

Do not allow any of it to allow you to think my memory is short. It simply means I do not need to discuss it for it to be felt by you at the appropriate time.

I Am Not Elastic

Life has taught me to take things one day at a time.

It has been a great lesson to learn.

People expect you just snap back after things that affect people you love or yourself.

I am not elastic. I do not just pop back into the shape I was in before the hurt, pain, tears and acceptance.

My skin is beautiful and the melanin will stay popping but underneath it is a person with a real soul struggling to understand it all.

Please stop telling me how strong I am.

I am forced to be strong but when do we force ourselves to heal?

Shaken

Life is coming at us hard and fast.

We do not have time to recover from one situation before we are struggling through the next one.

I am starting to view it as if it we are living in a time of determining our type of tree and the type of trees that surround us.

Strong winds and fierce storms are wreaking havoc everywhere and as we look around, we are seeing the trees being shaken.

Notice that some leaves are being blown away while others hold on but then branches start breaking.

Notice trees are being split, destroyed and even burned.

One thing I have started to notice are the roots.

Some trees are being pulled up with the roots
while others are being destroyed yet the roots
remain untouched.

The roots… It's all in the roots.

The foundation…

I, personally, am okay with being shaken but my
roots are what I am always trying to ensure are
untouched.

#shepherd #australianbuloke #redoak
#redmulberry #Ficusbengalensis #oak #maple
#elm #ash #sequoia #shakenbutnotdestroyed

Unmoved

42

Fear is the fare the enemy tries to charge us for our faith. We must absolutely never pay it. No matter how mighty the storm may seem, sleep in the boat with JESUS. You are protected!!!

Fear has never created an environment that my faith in JESUS has not seen me through in this life!!!

What He Has Taught Me…

I have been making personal and professional decisions/adjustments.

I am finally in a place where "Bag Lady" is not applicable to me.

I have been fortunate enough to have another person in my Circle who encourages me, holds me accountable and inspires me to think outside of my personal comfort zone.

He is quick to say "Oh hell nawl." if someone tries to hurt me.

He was the person I called on when I was in a place where I required medical assistance and he moved the earth to get it.

He is unapologetic in loving me.

He has taught me how to laugh at clowns and then read them so nicely they remove their own makeup so they become a student of the teacher.

He has taught me to stand up for myself and do
not accept mistreatment from anyone.

He has taught me love in ways I never
understood.

He has taught me acceptance in ways the world
does not want us to accept.

He has taught me that getting it out the mud was
the best way to ever get it because it keeps me
where I need to be to do what I do.

He has taught me to stop apologizing to people
who owe me apologies.

He has taught me that pressing on and refusing
to fold is a requirement. One we meet humbly
and passionately.

He has taught me that being underestimated is
the absolute greatest gift anyone can give you
because they will never really see you coming.

He has taught me food, laughter and friends are
very important and necessary.

He has taught me that it is okay to lean on those
who love you.

He has taught me that to practice the very things
you speak will provide the greatest proof that
love and compassion win.

He has taught me…

He has taught me…

He has taught…

And then he taught me how to walk away…

He taught me goodbye.

Soar high, Doctor!!! The world deserves your
brilliance.

#BeforeYourTime
#LoveUnconditional
#WalkIntoYourDestiny
#TheDoctor

My Tears Are Because Of You and A Celebration Too

It is in part because of your dreams that we are living our own!!!

You raised the bar for each of us and refused to accept us not surpassing it.

You have this amazing belief in me. "She can do anything she sets out to do."

Did I fail you?

I truly know I did not disappoint you.

"I love you. You will always be my Banana Box. Plus, you are my favorite niece."

"I love you too!!! You will always be my favorite uncle. I am your only niece."

"Oh yeah but you would still be my favorite even if you were not the only one."

You told me to never settle in any way and I still refuse to settle.

The books, awards, appointments, businesses,
doors I earned the right to open, tables I sit at
that shift to me, etc al, are just a small part of the
things you wanted to ensure the world knew
about me.

You made sure they knew I am loved.

You did all you could do on this earth and GOD
has said it is time for you to rest.

Even in leaving us, you gave us time to prepare.

You understood you were going to gain but you
also knew we would feel your loss in every way
possible.

We will continue to ensure our children receive
everything we received from you and reap the
benefits of all you instilled in us.

Thank you for the gift of your love,
encouragement, support, understanding and
teachings!!!

Every beautiful memory I have of you will be
with me forever and I will continue to share
them with all of my children.

You planted seeds that found fertile ground and Unc, what a harvest you have left for us!!!

I love you!!!

This is not goodbye. I will see you again!!!

Rest.

Yes, I am crying but I am celebrating you too!!!

Finished

Yesterday was yesterday and I watched everything die.

I buried it all including hope, trust, respect, love, desire and dreams.

I watched the casket close and be lowered into the ground.

I stayed to witness the dirt being thrown in to cover it up.

I stood alone with tears streaming down my face as I accepted what has occurred. This final blow to my heart and soul that guarantees I am unavailable in the ways I once understood.

Weak… Manipulation… Evil… Unfaithful…

They changed me.

I stayed until the night turned to day because I knew when I turned and walked away, I would have nothing left to say.

The time has come to share my life.

It is time to allow others to watch and hear it all.

It is time.

I feel nothing.

When the stories are told all will know the truth.

I did not leave.

I did not make the decision.

I just opened my hand and let go because
holding on was causing me to bleed.

Unpacking Yourself

51

When you really do the difficult work of
breaking strongholds, refusing to lie to yourself
anymore, being very intentional about growing
as well as becoming a better person and
releasing…

I have come to realize I have a loyalty to those I
love but most of them do not have it for me.

I have come to accept I have extraordinary love
for those I am loyal to in my life.

Both my unconditional loyalty and unwavering
love have been weaponized against me because I
refused to change who I was in hope that those I
gave it to would one day love me the way I
loved them.

They understand everything that comes to me
stays with me and will not be repeated.

I will protect them at all cost even if that means I
lose people I love in the end.

They have a sense of security with me I have
never had in life.

They continue on living their lives unbothered
while I hold all of them in me struggling to
figure out ways to help them heal, feel safe, stop
hurting, know loved, be understood, know they
are valued and realize they are always heard.

While they purposefully allow others to believe I
am the villain.

It was only today when I finally accepted on this
journey of getting me together I refuse to
continue down this path of pain that rips me
apart over and over again each time one of these
people I have been unquestionably loving and
loyal to in life decides to show me how little I
matter.

And today another part of me broke so it can
heal properly.

I Paid the Price In Full With No Discounts…

Staring in the mirror asking the person looking back at me the same question I have been asking her.

"Was it worth it?"

She never answers me but this time she plays my life for me.

I see the faces of the people who helped mold me into the person I am today.

I see the events that caused me to see people and this world the way I see it.

I see the births of my oldest son all the way down to my youngest child.

I see the memories and love I was blessed to share with them.

I see the opportunistic people who have unquestionably created strife and division for their own gain.

I see all I poured into my heartbeats only to see
how much I purposely hid from them so they
only saw the good in the very people who
constantly cover my name in blood.

I see the ways in which my oldest three sons will
be better men than the ones they think they
know and it is because I refused to accept less.

As tears flow down my face, I see the loss of my
children because they chose a side without me
providing them with straight truth and facts.

Was it worth it?

Absolutely. Each of them exist and will
contribute to this earth in positive ways that
supersedes the things they do not know or
understand.

I may have paid the price in the end but I would
do it all over again for them!!!

Who You Are Matters…

55

I lost the real me attempting to adjust to disappointments, hurts, abuse, lies and conditional things around me.

I lost the real me dealing with people who were not my people.

Read that part again.

I put the real me on a shelf so I did not feel anything.

It made me better at existing but I stopped living.

Then came the storm…

I have learned it is okay to not be okay. I grieve people I love and have lost.

I realized I am lost and am learning to feel again in ways I stopped feeling.

Feelings made me weak or so I believed at the time.

Feelings allowed people to hurt and use you.

Forgiveness made you foolish.

Now I understand all of these things and more make me better as a person.

I am reminded of all the things that made me the person I loved and decided I need her to truly exist in life.

Being able to turn off my emotions is a tool of survival but I am not truly living.

If you see me smiling, you do not need to wonder what happened.

I am simply living and enjoying my life.

If you hurt me, I forgive you.

If I hurt you, I pray you forgive me.

I want both of us to eat. We are just not eating together.

How Am I Doing It?

Peace

Loving
Joy
Healing
Living Freely
Never Doubting My Value Again
Understanding A Loving Touch
Being Thankful For My Blessings
Walking Away From Anyone Unhealthy To Me

#TwoPeopleChangedMe
#GlowUp
#HiMyNameIs
#CollectionComingSoon

Morning Testimony...

When you are reflecting on your life as you are getting on an elevator and you hear...

"Sometimes it's better to have taken the stairs to get where you are going."

Message:

Don't try to ride the elevator when you are meant to take the stairs. It's not just about getting there. It's about what you are supposed learn and discern as you make your way to your destination.

You may work a little harder. You may become tired. You may sweat a lot. You may shed some tears. You may get angry and frustrated. You may even look around and see people that you thought were taking the stairs with you no where in sight. You may even want to give up or turn around.

But GOD!!!

Here are two questions...

How do you know that elevator would have
taken you where you truly needed to go?

How do you know you would have been
prepared for what you faced when you stepped
off the elevator?

#FasterIsNotAlwaysBetter
#TheJourney
#TheTestimony
#ItWasNecessary
#PraiseHim

Gratitude

Thank you for ensuring I became the woman I was destined to be in life.

Thank you for ensuring the person who saw the world through the lens of a child no longer exists.

Thank you for making me understand loyalty isn't just a word and for those I'm loyal to they know I'm forever loyal.

Thank you for allowing me to understand people play games even when you tell them you don't play.

Thank you for teaching me that #1 is the only place I am supposed to be in the life of the one who professes to love me.

Thank you for teaching me that age doesn't make you a man or woman. Wisdom and knowledge does it.

Thank you for teaching me that walking away and never looking back is okay.

Thank you for betraying me because without betrayals I wouldn't have ever found me.

Thank you for making me finally take a look at the person you see in this picture and see her natural beauty inside and out.

Thank you for being a part of my amazing Circle which consists of people who love me, will protect me and block out all of the noise when I need silence.

Thank you for loving me as if I were your child from the day we connected.

Thank you all for being a part of the reason I found me.

Saying Goodbye…

People look at you and have no idea what it took for you to get to the place you are in at this moment.

They also can't comprehend why you won't allow them to be the reason you regress!!!

They will never understand why you will not accept their mind games and blatant disrespect.

They will not understand why you refuse to not speak the truth and are unwilling to paint pretty pictures in the midst of a nightmare.

The joy and peace you've found will anger them.

They will try to threaten you and play mind games with you.

They won't understand why you stop responding. They won't understand but you do.

All that matters is you understanding.

S.T.R.A.P.

When you find yourself in these situations,
remember to do the following:

Stop
Think
Realize
Accept
Pivot

For the person who asked me to write something
to help them in the midst of their journey.

Three Powerful Women…

64

Today, I choose to celebrate three powerful women who helped me to dare to be great!!!

I've been fortunate in my life to meet some powerful, world renown and life changing women.

I have taken the wisdom they shared with me and honored their requests.

I have honored the things they helped me to find within myself and understand those things are me.

They lit fires within me to do things without fear of any pushback.

They taught me that I would have time to rest and be afraid when I was dead!!!

With all of the powerful people who have and continue to pour into my life, there are three powerful women I want to say thank you to because they were and still are my greatest motivation.

1. Aunt B… You gave me a gift that also turned out to hold the best kept secrets. You put a book in my hands at such an early age most people didn't understand the reason behind it.

You didn't stop there after giving me the book. You taught me to not only read but comprehend every single word on the page!!!

You taught me that words are powerful. You made me want to learn more, do more, grow more, become more, think more, change more and most importantly, make you proud.

2. Aunt T… You showed me the strength of a woman in ways I didn't understand as I witnessed them and it was only as I would become older that I would truly appreciate the woman you are on this earth.

$19… $19… $19… And a demand that I conquer the world and do great things.

You believed in me.

I pray I haven't disappointed you but I also want you to know I'm not finish.

3. The third woman is no longer on this earth but she is with me every single day.

I mourn her daily and the true impact of losing her can only be understood by those close enough to me to truly understand I lost me on when I lost her.

She is the only person I would hold a truth from for twenty seven years that was so traumatizing to me. I loved her more than I loved myself.

I wanted to give you the opportunity to experience the world without the stress of your life but you left me before I could give it to you.

I kept thinking let me do this one thing because I wanted her to know all that she sacrificed was not in vain.

She would smile because she knew I wasn't wasting my opportunities.

I regret not taking time when you told me to "Bring those babies down here in the summer. They will have me up and walking before you know it."

Then you laughed that laugh of yours.

You were excited about the thought of being able to cook for them and watch them eat. Momma, they are eating everything in sight now, so your garden and cooking would be a gift now 🤍!!!

I didn't get a summer. They get to hear me laugh and talk about you.

They still don't believe you may have driven ten miles an hour maximum.

Mom, as painful as it is, they watch me grieve. They have watched me change. They are watching me hurt and at one time, they watched me just be angry.

Mom, I pray I made you proud while you were here and I pray I continue to make you proud.

Your work was not wasted. I'm a testimony.

Today, I salute my three beautiful, brave and brilliant powerful influencers.

I love all three of you!!!

Everything I have done, am doing or will do is because of the three of you!!!

Thank each of you!!!

Everything Is Within

Within peace lies every beautiful thing we will ever need or desire.

The word is often said but I do not think its value is truly understood or appreciated.

Peace removes the pressures of life which normally create anxiety, depression, hurt, disappointment, etc al.

Peace allows you to simply be in the moment.

You watch your babies grow with joy not sadness.

Lego time, with your son, is fun even when you step on one afterwards (OUCH!).

Tea time, with your daughter, is relaxing even if you never get to choose your seat.

You do not stress over who will be the person sharing your life or your bed.

You enjoy relaxing conversations, laughter, story time, lunch and even memories.

It is all found through peace.

The power in peace is my blessing and I am thankful I found it.

It allows me to move differently.

Peace also comes through ensuring I do not disturb another person in their peaceful space.

Communication is key.

When communicating make sure both of you have the same expectations.

Here are some examples:

Dinner is dinner.

Making love once is simply once.

Conversation is conversation.

I do not have time for anything more than this right now.

I want more than this with you.

Right now, I just need an orgasm.

I really enjoyed laughing and talking with you today.

Whatever the communication, just be clear and honest.

If you are unable to agree, walk away from it because it is not worth your peace.

No false hopes or expectations.

It all leads you to… PEACE!!!